GROSS ENOUGH TO WAKE THE DEAD. . . .

What's the difference between boogers and broccoli?

Kids don't eat broccoli.

———————

What did Mike Tyson say to Don King after the Holyfield fight?

"Damn. They really do taste like chicken."

———————

Why couldn't the Greek guy go bobbing for apples?

His sister was using the toilet.

———————

Why do Mexicans eat refried beans?

To get a second wind.

———————

How many lawyers does it take to stop a moving bus?

Not enough.

BOOK YOUR PLACE ON OUR WEBSITE AND MAKE THE READING CONNECTION!

We've created a customized website just for our very special readers, where you can get the inside scoop on everything that's going on with Zebra, Pinnacle and Kensington books.

When you come online, you'll have the exciting opportunity to:

- View covers of upcoming books
- Read sample chapters
- Learn about our future publishing schedule (listed by publication month *and author*)
- Find out when your favorite authors will be visiting a city near you
- Search for and order backlist books from our online catalog
- Check out author bios and background information
- Send e-mail to your favorite authors
- Meet the Kensington staff online
- Join us in weekly chats with authors, readers and other guests
- Get writing guidelines
- AND MUCH MORE!

**Visit our website at
http://www.zebrabooks.com**

FRIGHTFULLY GROSS JOKES

Volume XXX

Julius Alvin

Zebra Books
Kensington Publishing Corp.

http://www.zebrabooks.com

ZEBRA BOOKS are published by

Kensington Publishing Corp.
850 Third Avenue
New York, NY 10022

First Printing: October, 1999
10 9 8 7 6 5 4 3 2 1

Printed in the United States of America

Contents

Contents

NOW THAT'S GROSS

Gladys and Fanny were old maid sisters—both virgins. One day Gladys says to Fanny, "I'm not going to die a virgin. I'm going out and not coming back until I get laid!"

True to her word, she leaves at sundown, and by midnight, Fanny is getting worried. Finally, a little after two, the front door flies open and Gladys runs in—making a beeline for the bathroom.

Fanny knocks on the bathroom door. "Are you all right, Gladys?" she asks.

No answer. Fearing the worst, Fanny opens the door and there sits Gladys on the toilet, with her panties down around her ankles, her legs spread, her head stuck between her legs looking at something.

"What on earth are you doing?" Fanny wants to know.

"Sister," Gladys says, "it was ten inches long when it went in . . . and five inches when it came out. When I find the other half, are you gonna have the time of your life!"

———————

The blonde was baking up a batch of cookies for her boyfriend when the house caught on fire. Rushing to the phone, she dials 911.

"Help," she tells the operator. "My house is on fire!" Send the fire department!"

"Okay," says the operator. "How do we get to your house?"

"Duh!" the blonde says. "In the big red truck!"

Two guys—one married, one single— are discussing life. The single one says to his friend, "How's your sex life after twenty years of marriage?"

The married man responds, "We've been into S&M for some time."

"S&M?" the single guy asks.

"Yeah." says the married guy. "I snore and she masturbates."

———————

What happens when a blonde puts her panties on backward?

She gets her ass chewed out.

What's the most popular bra size in the nursing home?

Thirty-eight long.

———

How can you tell when your house has been burglarized by a homo?

All your jewelry is missing and your furniture has been tastefully rearranged.

———

What does a lawyer use for birth control?

His personality.

What do you get when you lock a fag and a Jew in a closet?

A musical.

———————

Why do you fuck sheep on the edge of a cliff?

The sheep push back harder.

———————

What did the lawyer say when he stepped in dog shit?

"Oh, my God—I'm melting!"

Did you hear about the Polish wolf?

He chewed three of his legs off and he was still caught in the trap.

———————

What do you find inside a clean nose?

Fingerprints.

———————

What's the difference between a computer and a woman?

The computer will take a three-inch floppy.

How do New York women get rid of cock-roaches?

They ask them for a commitment.

———————

What do a condom and a wife have in common?

They both spend most of their time in your wallet.

A Lutheran minister is driving on the highway and is pulled over for speeding. The state trooper says to him, "Do you know how fast you were going, sir?"

The minister doesn't. The trooper smells alcohol on the minister's breath, then sees an empty wine bottle on the floor.

"Sir," the trooper asks, "have you been drinking?"

The minister replies, "Only water."

"Then why do I smell wine?" the trooper asks, pointing to the bottle.

The minister says, "Good Lord, He's done it again!"

FIVE REASONS YOU CAN'T GET A JOB

1. You list *smoking weed* as a hobby on the job application.

2. Instead of shaking hands, you ask them to pull your finger.

3. Slashed *coworkers with knife* doesn't look good on your resume.

4. Narrow-minded personnel people find *alien abductions* unacceptable explanation for gaps in your job history.

5. You list fifth grade as your senior year.

What's the last thing you want to hear your grandmother say?

"Come in here and look at this before I flush!"

———————

How do lawyers sleep?

First they lie on one side, then on the other.

———————

The doctor says to the old man, "I need a urine sample and a stool sample and a semen sample."

The old man replies, "I'm in a hurry. Can't I just leave a pair of underpants?"

How many psychiatrists does it take to screw in a lightbulb?

What do *you* think?

FIVE THINGS MEN SHOULD NEVER SAY AT VICTORIA'S SECRET

1. Does this come in children's sizes?

2. No, thanks. Just sniffing.

3. Mom will love this.

4. No need to wrap it. I'll eat it here.

5. Oh, honey, you'll never squeeze your fat ass into that!

A drunk staggers into a Catholic church and makes his way into the confession box. He says nothing.

The bewildered priest coughs to catch the man's attention, but the man stays silent. The priest then knocks on the wall three times in a final attempt to get the man to speak.

Finally, the drunk replies, "No use knocking, pal. There's no toilet paper in this one either.

———

"I have good news and bad news," the defense lawyer says to his client.

"What's the bad news?" the client asks.

"The bad news is," the lawyer says, "the blood test came back. Your DNA is the exact match found at the murder scene."

"What's the good news?"

"Well," the lawyer says, "your cholesterol is down to 140."

So the sergeant was instructing the Polish paratrooper before his first jump.

"Count to ten and pull the rip cord,"the sergeant tells the Polack. "If that doesn't work, pull the second rip cord for the auxillary chute. After you land, a truck will pick you up."

The Polack jumps out of the plane, counts to ten, and pulls the first rip cord. Nothing happens. He pulls the second cord, and nothing happens again.

The Polack says to himself, "I bet the truck won't be there either!"

———————

Two black kids are playing in the schoolyard. The first one says, "My dad knew he was going to die two months before he did!"

"How did he know that?" the second kid asks.

The first black kid replies, "The judge told him!"

Hear about the Polish car insurance?

It's called "my fault."

––––––––––

What do Yuppies call oral sex?

Sixty-something.

––––––––––

Why do lawyers love playing golf?

It's the only time they get to dress up like pimps.

How can you tell when your roommate is gay?

His dick tastes like shit.

_____

Why did the woman cross the road?

Who gives a shit? Why isn't she in the kitchen?

_____

What's a female bisexual?

A lesbian with car trouble.

A man and his pet monkey walk into a bar. The man orders a beer. The monkey goes crazy, tearing the place apart. The bartender says nothing. The man and the monkey leave.

The next day, the man and the monkey come back to the bar. The man orders a beer as his monkey proceeds to jump onto the pool table and eat the cue ball. The bartender says, "That does it. Take your damn monkey and don't come back!"

The day after that, the man and the monkey return to the same bar. The bartender says, "I thought I told you two not to come back."

The man replies, "Oh, it's okay, bartender. The monkey learned his lesson."

The bartender leaves it at that. Just then the monkey jumps onto the bar and grabs a big olive. The monkey shoves the olive up his ass, then pulls it out and eats it.

The bartender is repulsed. He says, "Did you see what your monkey just did with that olive?"

"I'm sorry," the man says. "Ever since he ate that cue ball, he measures everything."

Why did the condom fly across the room?

It got pissed off.

————————

What is the NRA's new slogan?

"Guns don't kill people. O.J. does."

A guy gets a free ticket to the Super Bowl from his company. When he gets to the stadium, he realizes that his seat is in the last row of the stadium. At halftime, he notices an empty seat right behind the fifty yard line. He sneaks past the security guard into the empty seat. He asks the old gentleman sitting next to him, "Excuse me, but is this seat taken?"

The old man says, "Well, it actually belongs to me. I was supposed to come with my wife, but she just died. This is the first Super Bowl we haven't spent together in thirty years."

The guy says, "That's terrible. Couldn't you get a relative or a friend to come with you?"

"I tried," the old man says, "but they were all at the funeral."

How can you tell a WASP teenager?

The alligator on his shirt has zits.

————————

Why do doctors and nurses wear masks during an operation?

If somebody fucks up, nobody will know them.

————————

Why did the woman stick a candle up her cunt?

Her boyfriend liked to eat by candlelight.

A woman has a heart attack and almost dies on the operating table. During her near death experience, she sees God and asks him, "Is it my time yet?"

God responds, "No. You have another forty years to live."

The woman recovers and figures, since she's got forty more years to live, she might as well have a facelift, liposuction, and a tummy tuck. As she walks out of the hospital, she's killed by a runaway ambulance. She goes up to heaven and says to God, "I thought I had another forty years left."

God says, "Yes, but I didn't recognize you."

TRULY GROSS

What's the best thing about a blow job?

The ten minutes of silence.

———————

The guy bursts into the house and yells, "Pack your bags, honey. I just won the lottery for ten million dollars!"

His wife says, "Wonderful! Should I pack for the beach or the mountains?"

He responds, "I don't care . . . just get the fuck out."

Why do political sex scandals always involve Democrats?

Who would risk their career for a piece of elephant?

————————

What happened when the flasher decided to retire?

He decided to stick it out for another year.

————————

What's the smartest thing to ever come out of a woman's mouth?

Albert Einstein's dick.

What's the definition of a vagina?

A box that a penis comes in.

———————

How do you save your wife from drowning?

Take your foot off her head.

———————

What's the difference between a coffin and a cello?

The coffin has the dead guy on the inside.

———————

What's the last thing a guy wants to hear in a men's room?

"Nice cock."

What's the true definition of a gentleman?

Someone who can play the accordion, but doesn't.

———————

Why do blondes like cars with sunroofs?

More leg room.

———————

What's the difference between a blonde and a parrot?

A parrot can say no.

Hitler goes to see an astrologer and asks her, "When will I die?"

The astrologer says, "You will die on a Jewish holiday!"

Hitler cries, "A Jewish holiday? How do you know?"

The astrologer responds, "Any day you die will be a Jewish holiday."

———————

How does a pregnant lady know when she's carrying a future lawyer?

She has a craving for bologna.

What's the difference between *worry* and *panic?*

About twenty-eight days.

———————

What's the difference between an oral thermometer and a rectal thermometer?

The taste.

———————

What's the difference between boogers and broccoli?

Children won't eat broccoli.

What's the worst thing to throw to a drowning guitar player?

His amplifier.

———————

How do you make God laugh?

Tell Him your plans for your life.

———————

What's the difference between a duck and a lawyer.

A duck can shove a bill up its ass; the lawyer *should*.

Why do men give names to their cocks?

They have to take orders from someone.

———————

President Clinton and the Pope die at almost the same time—only the Pope is sent to hell and Clinton is sent to heaven. It takes St. Peter an hour to correct the mixup.

On his way back up to heaven, the Pope passes Clinton, who's headed in the opposite direction.

The Pope asks Clinton, "Where are you going?"

"Downstairs," Clinton replies. "Where are you going?"

"To see the Virgin Mary," the Pope says.

"Forget it," Clinton says. "You're twenty minutes too late."

The young woman says to her doctor, "Doc, I'm getting married this weekend and my fiance thinks I'm a virgin. Is there anything you can do to help me?"

"Medically, not really," the doctor replies. "Try this: On your wedding night, when you're getting ready for bed, slide a thick rubber band around your upper thigh. When your husband enters you, snap the rubber band and tell your husband it's your cherry popping."

On the wedding night, the new bride undresses in the bathroom and slips the rubber band around her thigh. She and her husband begin to make love. As her husband enters her, she snaps the rubber band right on cue.

"What the hell was that?" the husband asks.

"That was just my cherry snapping," the bride says.

"Well snap it again," her husband yells. "It's got my balls!"

What's the definition of a crying shame?

A busful of lawyers going off a cliff—and three seats are empty.

What's the worst thing about being an atheist?

When you are getting a blow job, you have nobody to talk to.

What's the difference between a violin and a cello?

A cello takes longer to burn.

———————

What do you call babies in a whorehouse?

Brothel sprouts.

———————

A little kid comes home and says to his mother, "Mommy, I want to be a musician when I grow up!"

His mother replies, "Well, you can't do *both*."

What's the name of the disease that paralyzes a woman from the waist down?

Marriage.

———————

How can you tell when a woman is having an orgasm?

Who cares?

———————

What's an Irish porno movie?

One minute of sex and fifty-nine minutes of whiskey commercials.

What is the ultimate rejection?

When your hand has a headache.

_____

How do you know when the female bartender doesn't like you?

There's a string hanging out of your Bloody Mary.

FIVE INDICATIONS YOU'RE A RED-NECK?

1. You have your wedding reception at the waffle house.

2. You spit on your own floor.

3. You had a receding hairline in the sixth grade.

4. You have three first names.

5. Your garbage man doesn't know what goes and what stays.

A priest is called away on an emergency. Not wanting to leave his confessional unattended, he calls his friend the rabbi from across the street and asks the rabbi to cover for him. The rabbi is happy to oblige, but tells the priest he doesn't know the procedure.

"No problem," the priest says. "Just watch what I do and then do the same."

Right then, a woman comes into the confessional and says, "Forgive me, Father, but I have committed adultery."

"How many times?" the priest asks.

"Three times," the woman replies.

The priest says, "Say two Hail Marys, put five dollars in the box, and sin no more."

A few minutes later a man enters the confessional and says, "Father, forgive me, for I have sinned. I committed adultery three times."

The priest says, "Say two Hail Marys, put five dollars in the box, and sin no more."

By this time, the rabbi tells the priest that he's got the hang of it. The priest leaves. A few minutes later, a woman enters and says to the rabbi, "Forgive me, father, but I have sinned."

The rabbi asks, "What did you do?"

The woman replies, "I committed adultery."

The rabbi asks, "How many times?"

The woman responds, "Once."

"Then go do it two more times," the rabbi replies. "We're running a special this week—three for five dollars."

———————

What's the best way to avoid rape?

Beat off your attacker.

———————

What's the definition of a belly button?

A place a blonde puts her gum on the way down.

GROSS
CELEBRITY
JOKES

What does Marv Albert say on the first date?

"Wanna go out for a bite?"

———————

What happened to John Denver's career?

It took a nosedive.

What was John Denver's favorite drink?

Ocean Spray.

––––––––––––

What did President Clinton say about *Roe*
v. *Wade?*

"I think the Haitians better row because
they can't wade."

––––––––––––

Why do people take an instant dislike to
Hillary Clinton?

It saves time.

What did the Queen of England say when she heard Diana died in a car crash?

"Was Fergie with her?"

———————

What's the difference between Rush Limbaugh and a whale?

The sports coat.

———————

Did you hear that Ellen Degeneres and Brett Butler are doing a sitcom together?

It's called *Grace under Ellen.*

What was Gianni Versace's last line?

Chalk.

How does President Clinton feel about foreign affairs?

He doesn't know—he's never had one.

What's the difference between the old U.S. Army and the new U.S. Army?

In the old army, soliders got blown *out of* foxholes.

Hear about Mattel's new divorced Barbie?

She comes with half of Ken's stuff.

———————

Why was America so surprised at the Donald Trump/Marla Maples divorce?

If two things go together, it's maples and rich sap.

———————

Why was baby Jesus born in a stable?

His parents were in an HMO.

Hear about the new Timothy McVeigh breakfast special at Denny's?

They take white bread and fry it.

———————

What do Michael Jackson and the New York Yankees have in common?

They both need twelve year olds to score.

———————

What's the difference between Mother Teresa and Princess Di?

One was chaste until she died; the other was chased until she died.

Hear about the song Elton John wrote for Mother Teresa?

It's called "Sandal in the Wind."

———————

Hear about Ellen Degeneres's new house?

It has no studs—only tongue and groove.

———————

What's the difference between Marv Albert and Sharon Stone?

Marv Albert wears panties.

What did Marv Albert say when NBC gave him the pink slip?

"No, thanks—already have one!"

———————

What's the difference between a Metallica concert and the Tyson–Holyfield match?

After Metallica, there's ringing in your ears; after the fight, there's ears in the ring.

———————

What did Mike Tyson say to Don King after the big bout?

"They really do taste like chicken!"

Who is going to be Mike Tyson's next opponent?

Lorena Bobbitt—winner eats all.

––––––––––––

What did Evander Holyfield say to his barber?

"Take a little off the ears."

––––––––––––

What did President Clinton do when someone threw a beer at him?

It was a draft, so he dodged it.

Hear about the new Bill Clinton doll?

Wind it up and it never tells the same story twice.

———————

THE FIVE SHORTEST BOOKS IN THE WORLD

1. *Al Gore—The Wild Years*

2. *Mike Tyson's Guide to Dating Etiquette*

3. *The Amish Phone Book*

4. *George Foreman's Big Book of Baby Names*

5. *Career Opportunities in Bosnia*

Why are Baptists boycotting *The Flintstones*?

They refuse to have a gay old time.

——————

Why did Michael Jackson fire Boyz II Men as his opening act?

He thought they were a delivery service.

Bill and Hilary Clinton are asleep one night in the White House. At two a.m. Hilary starts shaking Bill until he wakes up.

"What did you wake me up for?" Bill wants to know.

Hilary says, "I have to go to the bathroom."

Bill responds, "Why did you wake me up just to tell me that?"

Hilary says, "Because I want you to save my spot until I get back."

Adam is walking around the Garden of Eden, looking sad and lonely. God says to him, "What's the matter, Adam?"

Adam replies, "I haven't got anyone to talk to."

God says, "I think you need a woman, Adam."

"What's a woman?" Adam asks.

God says, "Someone who will cook for you and have your children and clean the house and give you sex whenever you want it, and she'll never have a headache and agree with every decision you make and be perfect in every way."

"I see," Adam says. "What exactly is this going to cost me?"

God replies, "An arm and a leg."

Adam thinks for a moment and says, "What can I get for just a rib?"

Why are presidents like diapers?

They need to be changed frequently—and for the same reason.

―――――――――

What does it mean when the American flag is flying at half mast at the post office?

Now Hiring.

―――――――――

What's twelve inches long and hangs in front of an ass?

Newt Gingrich's tie.

What do you call Newt Gingrich and President Clinton sitting in the front seat of your car?

Dual air bags.

————————

How did John Denver learn to fly a plane?

He took a crash course.

————————

What was the last thing that went through John Denver's mind before he crashed?

The propeller.

Why is it a tragedy that John Denver died?

Madonna wasn't with him.

―――――

What's the difference between Cheerios and the Dallas Cowboys?

Cheerios belong in a bowl.

―――――

Two Dallas Cowboys are riding in a car. Who's driving?

The cop.

Hear that the Dallas Cowboys just adopted a new honor system?

It goes: "Yes, your honor. No, your honor."

Who is the Dallas Cowboys' new defensive coach?

Johnnie Cochran.

Why did the Unabomber move to the Middle East?

He wanted to be less conspicuous.

What were Gianni Versace's last words?

"No, you can't have it with blue buttons!"

What's the difference between Evander Holyfield and corn?

Corn has ears.

Why was Jeffrey Dahmer picked as the spokesman for Oscar Meyer?

His bologna really did have a first name.

1986: President Reagan is in office and the White House buys new china.

1996: President Clinton is in office and China buys the White House.

―――――――

How did America celebrate Ronald Reagan's eighty-eighth birthday?

They forgot about it.

―――――――

Why was the price of a Big Mac raised ten cents?

So Ronald McDonald can stay in the Lincoln bedroom.

What's the name of Dr. Kevorkian's new rock album?

Unplugged.

_____

How many gangster rappers are there in America?

Depends when you ask—now, or ten minutes from now.

_____

What did the doctor say to Michael Jackson as he left the hospital with his newborn son?

"Hey—only one per father!"

What did President Clinton say to Ted Kennedy?

"At least mine are still alive when I'm done with them."

———————

How does Richard Gere get in shape for Groundhog Day?

He squats.

———————

Hear about Evel Knievel's new stunt?

He's driving a lunch wagon across Ethiopia.

GROSS RACIAL
JOKES

How do you know when you're flying on a Mexican airline?

When you get off the plane, you have to buy your luggage back.

A black kid comes home from school and says, "Mamma, guess what? I got the biggest cock in the third grade! Is it because I'm black?"

"No, honey," his mother says. "It's because you're sixteen."

How did the Germans capture Poland so easily?

They marched in backward and said they were leaving.

What does a black guy get when he picks his nose?

Noogers.

What do you call a black woman who's had three abortions?

Merciful.

What's the definition of busy?

One set of jumper cables at a Mexican wedding.

Why did the cannibal starve to death in Mexico?

He found plenty of food but he couldn't clean it.

What do you call a butler from India?

Mahat macoat.

———————

What did the black guy do when he won the lottery?

He bought a limousine and hired a white guy to sit in the back.

———————

How did the Polish mother get her kid to stop biting his nails?

She bought him a pair of shoes.

What's the difference between a Polack and a turd?

The color.

———————

Why did the black woman make it into the *Guinness Book of World Records*?

Her pussy was bigger than her husband's lips.

———————

Why don't white people fill out organ-donor cards?

They don't want to end up with a black lung.

What's big and brown and hairy and has big lips and fell off the Empire State Building?

Martin Luther Kong Jr.

———————

Why did the Polack get mad at his wife?

He was out shooting craps and she didn't know how to cook them.

———————

Why are Irish men like bumper stickers?

They're both hard to get off.

Hear about the Polack who won the lottery?

He gets a dollar a year for a million years.

———————

How long do folks from Alabama cook their meat?

Until the tire marks go away.

———————

What do you call a Mexican with a vasectomy?

A dry Martinez.

What's the difference between an African American and a piece of shit?

After a while, shit turns white and stops stinking.

———

So two old Jews meet on Broadway. Murray says to Sol, "So, Sol, what's new?"

Sol says, "Well, I just won twenty million dollars in the lottery."

"Twenty million?" Murray exclaims. "That's great. What are you going to do with the money?"

Sol responds, "I'm building a big monument to Adolf Hilter."

Murray is shocked beyond belief. "A monument to Hitler? Are you crazy? Why are you building a monument to Hitler?"

Sol says, "Well, he was nice enough to tattoo the winning lottery numbers on my arm."

HAIL TO THE CHIEF

What advice did Yassar Arafat give to President Clinton?

"Bill, remember—goats don't talk!"

———————

What's the difference between Gennifer Flowers, Paula Jones, Monica Lewinsky, and Hilary Clinton?

The first three like to sleep with men.

Why is Chelsea Clinton so angry at her father?

He's getting more dates than she is.

———————

What's the new Presidential anthem?

"Kneel to the Chief."

———————

What's the recipe for Bill Clinton Stew?

One small weenie in hot water.

Why shouldn't we feel sorry for Monica?

She'll be back on her knees in no time.

———————

What did Ted Kennedy say to Bill Clinton?

"Why didn't you just drive her home?"

———————

Seen on an Arkansas bumper sticker:

"Honk if you haven't had sex with Bill Clinton!"

What do Watergate and Zippergate have in common?

They both had Deep Throat.

SO GROSS EVEN WE WERE OFFENDED

What would happen if President Clinton was gay?

All the cigars in the White House would taste like shit.

So the couple had been married for fifteen years. One day they're in the backyard, and when the husband sees his wife bend over to pluck some weeds, he says, "You know, honey, you're really getting fat. I bet your butt is as big as the gas grill."

To prove his point, he gets his tape measure and goes to work. He measures the gas grill, then his wife's butt.

"Just as I thought," the husband says. "Just about the same size."

With this, the wife gets pissed off and doesn't talk to him for the rest of the day. That evening when they go to bed, the husband snuggles up to his wife and says, "How about a little lovemaking, honey."

The wife rolls over, giving her hubby the cold shoulder; then she says, "You don't think I'm gonna fire up my big grill for one little weenie, do you?"

An old farmer was hauling a load of horse manure when he was stopped by a state trooper. "You were speeding," the trooper says, "so I've got to give you a ticket."

"Yep," the farmer says, watching the cop swat away a bunch of flies.

"These flies are terrible," the trooper complains.

"Yep," the farmer says. "Them's circle flies."

"What the hell is a circle fly?" the trooper wants to know.

"Them's flies that circle a horse's tail," the old farmer says.

The trooper asks the farmer, "You wouldn't be calling me a horse's ass, would you, old man?"

"Nope," the farmer replies, "but you just can't fool them flies!"

What's the difference between a cowlick and a vaginal air burst?

One's a fussy part and the other's a pussy fart.

———————

What do you call a gay vegetable?

A lez-bean.

———————

What do you call a doctor who treats fat women's vaginas?

A rhinocologist.

Why couldn't the Greek guy go bobbing for apples?

His sister was using the toilet.

———————

What's invisible and smells like dirt?

A Somalian fart.

———————

What do you call a black bodybuilder?

Schwartzenigger.

TWELVE CHILDREN'S BOOKS YOU'LL NEVER SEE

1. *You Were an Accident*

2. *Strangers Have the Best Candy*

3. *The Little Sissy Who Snitched*

4. *Some Kittens Can Fly!*

5. *How to Dress Sexy for Grown-ups*

6. *Where Would You Like to Be Buried?*

7. *Katy Was So Bad Her Mom Stopped Loving Her*

8. *The Kid's Guide to Hitchhiking*

9. *Garfield Gets Feline Leukemia*

10. *What Is That Dog Doing to That Other Dog?*

11. *Why Can't Mr. Fork and Ms. Electrical Outlet Be Friends?*

12. *Daddy Drinks Because You Cry*

What do you call a retired black hooker?

Grandma.

_____

What do you put at the top of a Polish ladder?

STOP!

_____

What did one testicle say to the other testicle?

"It was Peter that did all the shooting. So why should we hang?"

How do you know you're getting old?

Your wife gives up sex for Lent and you don't find out till Easter.

———

So the cop pulls over a guy in a pickup truck filled with penguins.

"You can't drive around with penguins in the back of a truck! Take 'em to the zoo immediately!"

The guy says okay and drives off. The next day the cop sees the guy driving around and his pickup truck is still full of penguins—only this time they're all wearing sunglasses.

The cop pulls him over and says, "I thought I told you to take them penguins to the zoo."

"I did," the guy says. "And today I'm taking them to the beach."

What's the best alternative to marriage?

Find a woman you hate and buy her a house.

———————

Why is it better to be good to your kids?

They're the ones choosing the nursing home.

———————

What's the definition of fair?

If women have PMS, then men should have ESPN.

"I'm very sorry your wife passed away, Murray," a guy says to his friend. "losing a wife can be hard."

The friend replies, "Yes. in my case it was almost impossible."

———

What do you do when you run out of sick days at work?

Call in dead.

———

What's the state slogan of Kentucky?

Five Million People—Fifteen Last Names

A drunk staggers into the diner and orders some eggs. The waiter puts in the order and the cook says, "We're out of fresh eggs. All I got are two rotton ones."

The waiter says, "Give him the rotten eggs. He's so loaded he'll never know the difference."

The cook scrambles up the eggs, which are promptly served to the drunk. The drink devours them without comment.

Later, paying the check, the drunk asks the waiter, "Where do you get your eggs?"

The waiter replies, "We have our own chicken farm."

The drunk asks, "You got a rooster?"

"No," the waiter says.

"Then you better get one," the drunk says, "because some skunk is fucking your chickens."

Three old friends are driving home from a football game and all die in a smashup. They find themselves at an orientation session to enter heaven.

They are asked, "When you are in your casket and your family and friends are mourning you, what would you like to hear them say about you?"

The first friend replies, "I'd like to hear them say that I was a great doctor and a great family man."

The second friend replies, "I'd like to hear them say that I was a great father and husband and a schoolteacher who made a difference in the lives of our children of tomorrow."

The third guy says, "I would like to hear them say, 'Look, he's moving!'"

A guy in a ski mask bursts into a sperm bank wielding a shotgun. "Open the safe!" he yells at the girl behind the counter.

"But we're not a real bank!" she pleads. "We don't have money, only sperm!"

"Don't argue. Open the fucking safe or I'll blow your head off!"

She does. Then the intruder says, "Now, take out one of those little bottles and drink it!"

"But it's full of sperm!" she cries.

"Don't argue. Just drink it," he says, waving the shotgun at her.

She pries the lid off the bottle and gulps it down.

The guy pulls off his mask, and to the woman's amazement, it's her husband.

"There," he says to her. "That wasn't so difficult, was it?"

FIVE THINGS YOU'LL NEVER HEAR A MAN SAY

1. Here, honey, you take the remote.

2. While I'm up, can I get you anything?

3. She seems very nice, but her breasts are just too big.

4. Forget Monday Night Football. Let's just talk.

5. Sex isn't that important. I just like to be held.

FIVE THINGS YOU'LL NEVER HEAR A WOMAN SAY

1. This diamond is way too big!

2. Honey, does this outfit make my butt look too small?

3. Pull my finger!

4. Don't stop for directions. I'm sure you'll be able to figure out how to get there.

5. I don't care if it's on sale. Three hundred dollars is just too much for a designer dress.

What do Puerto Ricans use for wedding rings?

Flea collars.

———————

Why do Mexicans eat refried beans?

To get a second wind.

———————

How do you know when your girlfriend is really fat?

You have to take her to Sea World to get her baptized.

What do you get when you trade your wife for a skunk?

A better-smelling pussy.

What do old women have between their tits that young women don't?

A belly button.

What do you call diapers for old people?

Grampers.

Why are anchovies like telephones?

They're the next best thing to being there.

———————

What's the difference between a lawyer and a vulture?

Frequent flyer miles.

———————

A guy goes to see his doctor and says, "Doc, you gotta help me. I'm having trouble controlling my bladder."

The doctor replies, "Get off my carpet."

A little boy walks into his parents' bedroom while they're having sex. The little boy asks his mother, "What are you doing, Mommy?"

She replies, "Daddy is so fat I'm bouncing all the air out of him."

"I don't think that will do much good, Mommy," the boy says. "The lady next door will just blow him up again."

———————

Did you hear about the accident in Arkansas?

A doctor and two nurses fell off the scaffold while working on Paula Jones's nose.

———————

What was the first thing Paula Jones did with her first million dollars?

She bought a doublewide so she would have room to turn her head.

A guy phones a law firm and says, "I want to speak to my lawyer."

The receptionist replies, 'I'm sorry, but he died last week."

The next day, the guy phones the law firm and says, "I want to speak to my lawyer."

Again the receptionist replies, "I'm sorry but he died last week."

On the third day, the guy calls the law firm again and says, "I want to speak to my lawyer."

The receptionist, a little annoyed, says, "I keep telling you that your lawyer died last week. Why do you keep calling?"

The guy says, "Because, I just love hearing it!"

What's the definition of Branson, Missouri?

Las Vegas for the toothless.

————————

Two old people get married. On their wedding night, the old bride tells her groom, who's a little hard of hearing, "I've got acute angina."

"That's good," the old man replies, "because those are the saggiest tits I've ever seen."

When nuns are admitted to heaven, they go through a special gate and are expected to make one last confession before they become angels.

Several nuns are lined up at the gate, waiting to be absolved of their last sins before they are made holy.

"And so," St. Peter says to the first nun, "have you ever had contact with a penis?"

The first nun says, "Once I touched the top of one with the tip of my finger."

St. Peter says, "Dip your finger in the holy water and pass on to heaven." To the second nun, he asks the same question.

The second nun replies, "Once I got carried away and . . . sort of massaged one."

St. Peter replies, "Very well. Rinse your hand in the holy water and pass on to heaven."

Suddenly, there's some jostling in the line—one of the nuns is trying to cut in front. St. Peter asks, "What's going on here?"

The pushy nun says to him, "Sorry, St. Peter, but if I have to gargle that holy water, I wanna do it before Sister Mary sticks her ass in it."

What do Rosanne and a cocaine dealer have in common?

Three hundred pounds of crack.

―――――――

What do you call a homosexual with a chipped tooth?

An organ grinder.

―――――――

Why won't a woman ever win the Indy Five Hundred?

She always stops to ask directions.

Little Johnny goes to school, and the teacher says, "Today we are going to learn multisyllable words. Can anyone give me an example?"

Little Johnny waves his hand and cries, "Me, teacher, me!"

"Go head, Johnny," the teacher says.

Johnny says, "Mas-tur-bate."

The teacher replies, "Well, Johnny, that's quite a mouthful."

Johnny says, "No, teacher. You're thinking of a blow job. I'm talking about a hand job!"

GROSS GAY AND
LESBIAN JOKES

What do you get when you cross fifty lesbians and fifty Democrats?

A hundred people who don't do dick.

What do you call two lesbians in a rowboat?

Fur traders.

What happened when the transvestites were arrested?

They were charged with male fraud.

_____

What's the difference between a fag and a suppository?

Nothing.

_____

How many homosexuals does it take to screw in a lightbulb?

One—as long as there's plenty of K-Y and he's real careful.

What's the name of the organization of gay men who sexually abuse pigs?

Hambla.

_____

What's the gay definition of hemorrhoids?

Speed bumps.

_____

What was the name of the TV show that featured fags in a Nazi prison camp?

Hogan's Homos.

_____

What's a lesbian's favorite pet?

A lapdog.

A GROSS VARIETY

What do you call a lawyer with an IQ of fifty?

Your honor.

_____

What is the ideal weight for a lawyer?

About three pounds, including the urn.

What do you call a lawyer who's gone bad?

Senator.

_____

How many lawyers does it take to stop a moving bus?

Not enough.

What do you get for a friend who's graduating from law school?

A lobotomy.

———————

How do you save a lawyer from drowning?

Shoot him before he hits the water.

What do you call an aerobics instructor who doesn't cause pain and agony?

Unemployed.

_____

Why did the aerobics instructor cross the road?

Someone on the other side could still walk.

What do you do when your wife wants you to be more affectionate?

Get two girlfriends.

What's the definition of a jury?

Twelve people who decide which client has the better attorney.

THE TEN FAVORITE TV SHOWS IN IRAQ

1. *Husseinfeld*

2. *Allah McBeal*

3. *The Price Is Right If Saddam Says It's Right*

4. *Mad About Everything*

5. *Two Guys, a Girl, and a Fatwah*

6. *Everybody Loves Saddam or He'll Have Them Shot*

7. *My Two Baghdads*

8. *Iraq's Funniest Public Executions*

9. *Mohammed Loves Chachi*

10. *I Love Lucy*

Little Johnny is called on by his teacher during the math lesson. The teacher asks, "Johnny, if there were five birds sitting on a fence and you shot one with your gun, how many would be left?"

"None," Johnny answers, " 'cause the rest would fly away."

"Well, the answer is four," the teacher says. "But I like the way you're thinking."

Little Johnny says to the teacher, "I have a question for you. If there were three women eating ice cream cones, one licking her cone, one biting her cone, and the third one sucking her cone, which one is married?"

The teacher responds, "I guess the one sucking the cone."

"No," Johnny replies. "It's the one wearing the wedding ring. But I like the way *you're* thinking."

THE FIVE WORST THINGS TO SAY TO YOUR WIFE WHEN SHE'S PREGNANT

1. I ate all the Oreos.

2. I'm not implying anything, but I don't think the baby weighs forty pounds.

3. Got milk?

4. Are your ankles really supposed to look like that?

5. Can't they induce labor? The Super Bowl is next Sunday!